Words are weapons too! (Understanding the power of words)

Copyright © 2019 by Deetra La'Rue Benn

All rights reserved. No part of this book may be reproduced or transmitted in any form or by any means without written permission from the author. In need of some encouragement, hope and motivation? Visit and follow me at www.notesbylarue.com. For speaking engagements, workshops or business opportunities, please contact Deetra La'Rue at notesbylarue@gmail.com

ISBN 978-0-578-68985-2

## Dedication

I'd like to dedicate this book to all the people I have hurt, or have been hurt, particularly by someone they love and trust. I thank God for showing me the error of my ways, allowing me to grow and teaching me the true meaning of "Death and life are in the power of the tongue" (Proverbs 13:3). Words are deadly, and can kill your mental and emotional well-being, your self-esteem, your confidence, relationships, and so much more. Please use them carefully, because what may be nothing to you, is everything to someone else.

## Table of Contents

Chapter 1..........................................................Belle-wolf

Chapter 2.......................................................I'm sorry

Chapter 3..................................................You ruined it

Chapter 4.................................Words are weapons too

Chapter 5.......................................Sticks and stones

Chapter 6...............................................................Nancy

Chapter 7........................Are you uplifting or insulting?

Chapter 8............................Stop it before it harvests

Chapter 9...................................................Steel weak

Chapter 10.................................Silence is a response

Chapter 11.........................Walk, even if you are alone

Chapter 12..............Understanding the power of words

## Belle-wolf

"Shut up dummy, before you make me say something that I'll regret", are the words I can still hear echoing off the walls. I didn't like that voice, and more importantly, I didn't like the fact that it was mine. I'm sure you're shocked, just as much as I am. Knowing me, you probably wouldn't have guessed it, considering the fact that I pretended to be a Southern Belle, to guise that I was really a wolf, and a big bad one at that.

I didn't really care for one's feelings, or try not to hurt them, because that was my intent all along. Any and every little thing people did, bothered me, and as payback for their agitation, I would often unleash. In all reality, I was hurting on the inside, and I wanted others to feel the same. I was going through an abundance of problems, and I didn't know if I'd come out on top, or be buried underneath. Because I didn't know how to deal with my misery, I wanted others to keep me company. I'm a changed person now, and whoever reads this book, there's hope for you too. Allow me to show you!

## I'm sorry

Apologizing is never easy, especially when you feel as though you've done nothing wrong. However, I can honestly say, I have hurt quite a few people, and for that I am sorry. Coming from a person who used to think there were no error in her ways, that's a pretty big thing to admit. I used to have a very negative attitude, and that's nothing I am proud of, nor happy to state. If anything, I'm very embarrassed and disappointed in the woman I used to be, because I was better than my behavior, and I knew it.

There are a number of reasons (excuses) I could give for being who I was, but none of it matters, nor will ever make up for how I have talked to and treated people. I'd like to preface and say, I was by no means Cruella de Vil, but I wasn't an Angel either. Even as I sit and write this book, I'm finding it very hard to talk about the old me, because I can't fathom or understand why I acted in the manner in which I did. I've tried to find a rationale, but I can't seem to come up with one.

My thinking is quite torturous at times, because too often I beat myself up over the past, especially when I dwell on it for very long. I'd like to say I can't help who I was, but truth of the matter, I could have. Honestly speaking, I could have done a lot of things. I *could have* had a more pleasant attitude. I *could have* not said the harsh things that I said. I *could have* not treated people the way I did. More importantly, I *could have* chosen to walk away.

More times than plenty, I'm negative towards myself, and it's not a feeling I enjoy having. It sometimes makes me wonder, if this is what others have felt, as a result of my harshness. I realize my words and actions were very damaging, and although I can never take away the pain I've permanently left upon others, I can only hope they forgive me. I'm fully aware that an apology won't erase the hurt, but I'm hoping it'll at least soothe the pain. To all I have wronged or made feel anything other than good, I ask that you please forgive me and accept my sincerest apology!

I know you're probably saying, "Why now"? Or, "You're a day late and a dollar short", but I'd like to say, "I'm not late, but right on time", and so are you. If you are thinking of trying to make your wrongs a right, do it. Nobody can put a time limit on when you need to apologize, all that matters is that you get it done. One thing I will say though, just because you apologize doesn't mean they have to accept it. Some people have the mentality that, when you do them wrong, that's it, so don't look for any second chances.

They will cut you off, and tell you it's only because you handed them the scissors. In other words, it's all your fault. Regardless if they choose to forgive or hold a grudge, you have to be okay with whatever choice they make. Now, you may be thinking, the past should be in the past, or they should just let it go, but it's not that easy. I know all too well the art of letting things go is hard, because I'm still trying to master it myself. To be absolutely fair, when someone is hurting, you can't expect them to get over it, just because you have.

It takes months and years even, for people to let go of their pain, and some people simply don't. Before you get in your feelings and start saying things like, "I'm not going to beg anyone for forgiveness" or "I don't care if they accept my apology or not", you need to stop and put yourself in their shoes. How would you feel if someone said something hurtful to you? Do you think you would react any differently than them? If so, remember, not everyone is as resilient as you, so don't expect them to bounce back so quickly.

I have no qualms with doing what is right, or trying to mend anything or anyone that I have broken. That's my fault and I take full responsibility for my actions. I'm also fully aware that no matter how much I try to patch things together, there's a 100% chance I won't ever be able to put them back as they were, so I can understand if someone never wants to speak to me again. I've made a lot of mistakes and I know I'll make more, but one thing's for sure, intentionally hurting others won't ever be one of them. Besides, I've seen what that does to people, and let's just say, it's not something I want to be held responsible for.

## You ruined it

Have you ever received an apology from someone, but by the time they were done, it sounded more like an excuse? In their mind, they were expressing their sorrow as a result of their actions, but in all honesty, what they were doing was giving you a million and one reasons as to why it really wasn't their fault. For example, "I'm sorry I said those hurtful things to you, but it's only because you pushed my buttons".

It's so easy for people to misplace blame when they don't want to take responsibility for their actions. Rather than be mature and own up to their misdoings, they find a way to share the guilt. After all, had it not been for the other party involved, they wouldn't have been in that argument in the first place, right? You do know that just because someone invites you to a fight, it doesn't mean you have to accept the invitation?

Apologies are given all the time, but what's to be considered is whether or not you are truly sincere and genuine. In other words, did you really want to apologize and make things right, or were you only doing it, because someone told you too? Did you call them, speak with them in person, or did you opt to send it via text, because you weren't man or woman enough to face them?

To me, apologizing any way other besides in person or phone call, is one of the most ingenuine things you can do. I don't want to "read" that you are sorry, I need to hear it, see it and judge for myself if you really mean it. Besides, text messages can be perceived wrong at times, especially depending upon the person receiving it. What you feel you were saying, can actually be misconstrued and taken out of context.

Aside from the delivery of an apology, I honestly feel not giving one or thinking you shouldn't, is more hurtful than ruining it with an excuse. Sure, no one wants to feel as though they are wrong or have done anything wrong, but if you have, then you should be able to admit to your error and do whatever you can to correct it. Regardless of how small you feel the situation was, what's big is the impact it had upon that person.

You've got to realize, even though you feel as though that argument wasn't such a big deal, and it's not like "It's the end of the world", but to them, it probably is. One, they weren't expecting the hurt to come from you, and two you selfishly chose to disregard their feelings, thus letting them know how they feel is of little to no importance to you. "But, it shouldn't matter, because in a day or two, I'm sure they'll be over it".

That type of attitude is one of the most classic reasons why repeat offenders continue to do as they have. In their mind, "it's just words", but what they fail to realize is, "words can be pretty hurtful"! As a writer, I know how powerful and impactful my words are. People tell me all the time, how the things I've written has made them feel, so how do you suppose those you hurt are feeling? Before you ruin an apology with an excuse, think about what you're going to say. Will it add fuel to the fire, or put the one you started out? Whatever the outcome is, be prepared to deal with it.

**Words are weapons too**

When I think of a weapon, a gun is the first thing that comes to mind. Mainly, it's used for protection and to ward off potential offenders. However, words are weapons too! Obviously a gun is more deadly, but words can be too. Once spoken, there's nothing you can do or say to take them back. Yes, you can apologize and reiterate over and over again, how "you didn't mean it", but the pain remains.

As mentioned previously, I know the impact of my words, and they are my greatest ammunition. Like guns, I've often "mishandled" my weapon of mass destruction and "fired off" at the first person who had anything opposing to say. I didn't care if I missed or not, but because I was good at having a bad attitude, I had a 100% hit rate. Again, nothing to be proud of, but everything to be ashamed about.

There is this idea that "whatever comes up, is supposed to come out", but not if it's going to cause hurt, pain and dissension. Then again, "Who cares about division, when you're trying to prove a point to people and let them know why you shouldn't be messed with? However, the point I'm trying to make is this, if you have a rebuttal, do it with tact. There's nothing wrong with arguing your point, but don't use your disagreement as a chance for you to lodge attacks or hit below the belt.

You don't always have to say what's on your mind or feel compelled to speak. Sometimes, it's not what you say, but how you say it. We all know very well, that there are instances where we get caught up in the moment, and don't necessarily mean things we say, and I get that. I've been there too many times before, and when I got tired of being in that spot continuously, I made a point to not be there.

Instead, I chose my words carefully and made sure my delivery was in a way that my point was taken and I didn't cause offense. So many people are stubborn and unwilling to apologize, because to them they are accepting blame, and everybody knows, no one likes being blamed for anything, especially if they feel they didn't do anything wrong to begin with.

Words can either make or break you, and if you struggle with self-esteem issues, are sensitive or get offended easily, then you could potentially be destroyed. In fact, there are millions of people who are in situations they can't even pull themselves out of. They have been debilitated by others, because they've allowed what someone has said to determine their course of life, and ultimately, quality of it.

Take for instance a woman who is in a relationship that is not healthy for her. Every day, she is weakened by the verbal and mental abuse at the hands of her spouse or significant other. She's constantly told she's "dumb, stupid and won't ever amount to anything". Her self-esteem has taken a hit and because of the many blows she's received, she's fallen and is incapable of getting back up.

The one in whom she trusts, loves and considers to be her Superman, can't save her. Clearly caught in a matter of life and death, she's chosen the latter, because she isn't strong enough or equipped for survival. Ultimately, she loses her fight, because she's succumbed to every hurtful thing he has embedded in her head. Needless to say, she's depressed, can't get out of the bed, and just want to "give up", not realizing she already has.

How? How could a woman allow herself to fall victim to what someone says? After all, they're just words, right? Although he never physically abuses her, he was able to damage her mentally and emotionally, because he knew he could use something that would inflict pain, but not leave a physical mark. Fragile as she is, all he had to do was "just say something", because he knew she'd crumble. Now do you see why I say "words are weapons too"?

A person loses more than their self-esteem, confidence and self-worth, because of the hurtful and detrimental things people say. Their quality of life is gone, hopes, dreams, goals and ambition are taken away, because they've chosen what their abuser says as truth. Ultimately, they have reduced themselves to nothing, because it's what they were constantly told they are, so therefore, they must be.

You know, a lot of **hurt people**, have a tendency to hurt people, but that is no reason or justification for inflicting pain upon someone else, even though it was my excuse. In my previous books, I revealed how I accepted others thoughts and opinions of me, because of my low self-esteem and mental health issues. As a result of my battle with depression and anxiety, I always allow what others say and think of me, matter.

The invisible tape recorder of the hurtful things that people said to me, that only I could play and hear, drove me insane. I kept the insults and attacks on repeat, and even I don't know why. Eventually, it got too much for me to handle, so I started seeing a Therapist (amongst other reasons). Essentially, I gave control of my life over to those who hurt me, so I desperately needed help to regain not only control back, but my piece of mind and self-worth as well.

Almost a year into therapy, I've made progress, but let's just say, the emotional scars are still there. I used to tell myself that, "It doesn't matter what they say about me", when knowing all along, it did. I fight constantly to not care, be concerned or hurt by anything or anyone. However, I've chosen to get my life back and not obsess so much over someone else's thought or opinions of me, because that's how they feel.

I know it's pretty difficult to bounce back from unhealthy people and their toxic ways/words, but you need to make a point to tell yourself, those are their thoughts and feelings, so I don't have to own them, nor allow them to affect me. When they realize they can't get to you the way they used to, they'll bring out the big guns. They'll throw grenades of insults, hoping you'll blow up. When that doesn't work, they'll hit you extremely below the belt and bring you down to your knees, but get up, brush the dirt off and smile.

Just because they swing you, doesn't mean you have to swing back. I'm a blogger and one of my favorite bloggers, Dr. Eric Perry, wrote a post on the "Law of allowances". One of the most profound things he states is, "It is important to point out that the allowance of negative behaviors, from people in your life, is not because of a law of attraction but has everything to do with the law of allowances. What negative behaviors are you willing to allow from the people who surround you? It can be as simple as allowing a person to take a week to respond to your text. Or, it can be as serious as allowing abusive behaviors in your relationships".

The hurt and pain you experience from others, is allowed. You allow them to speak to you negatively, so they do. You allow them to treat you poorly, and they continue. When you allow people to devalue you, essentially you are saying, "I am worthless". One of the worst things you can do, is allow someone control over you and your emotions/feelings. In one of my many sessions with my Therapist, I'd often tell her how this person made me mad or made me act a certain way. In her not so motherly voice, she'd say, "A person will only do what you allow them to do, because you've given them control".

Although she can be a bit spicy at times in her delivery, it doesn't compare to the heat I've felt from others. I didn't realize what I was doing at the time, but now I know, I was giving my power away. Sad to say, I relinquished all control over to my enemies. When I regained my authority, I saw the benefits of turning a blind eye to them. Instead of fighting tic for tac with words, I didn't use any. I didn't give them any indication that what they said got to me. I did, however, give them something they never expected to receive, and that's me walking away.

Let's face it, people are so fucking mean. They'll find any reason to pick you a part, because of things they are unhappy with, but not willing to change. It's so sad that they'll ostracize you and enlarge your problems for the world to see, while minimizing theirs. It's not anything you've done wrong to them, but sometimes, people are mean, because they don't know how to deal with what they are going through. It could be the fact that they have no resilience, or was brought up in a home that didn't work through problems, but instead concealed them. Remember, a person don't know what to do in certain situations, because they were never taught how to handle them. Who knows, but what I do know is this, when I'm met with other's thoughts and negative feelings or words about me, I say to myself, "I would care, but this doesn't involve me"!

## Sticks and Stones

"Sticks and stones may break my bones, but words can never hurt me". I can still hear the chant echoed by my elementary school classmates. But, truth of the matter, words do hurt! A lot of power lie within the tongue, so when speaking to someone or about someone, be sensitive and extremely careful of what you say. I'm pretty sure we've all heard the saying, "If you don't have anything nice to say, then don't say anything at all".

People need to understand that just because you have a negative thought or the right to "speak your mind", doesn't mean you should say whatever comes to mind. Some people are incredibly sensitive, and even the smallest thing you say, can offend them. However, because I saw no fault in what I was doing, I figured they shouldn't take offense. When I realized they did, I wanted to use my words to inspire and be uplifting, not insulting. Although my careless use of words to retaliate against others temporarily made me feel better, it left them with an everlasting pain.

Knowing that makes me sad, because I'm the one that did it. Eventually, I had to learn that every action doesn't require a reaction. So now, when people speak negatively towards me, I let them. It took me a while to be able to take the high road, I'll admit. I had to remember that hurt people, hurt people. However, don't become one of those people. Always turn the other cheek and walk away. Be careful of your thoughts, because they turn into hurtful words and ultimately bad actions.

Remember, it's one thing to think it, but another when you release it, because there's no taking it back. It kind of reminds me of a balloon being let go, flying aimlessly away in the sky. Although you see it, you can't reach up and grab it back, because it's too far gone. The people you hurt are the balloons, and your negative words are the winds, which carries them away. No matter how much you apologize and try to make amends, some people won't ever come back, because they were completely "blown away" by what you said or did.

## Nancy

Sometimes, I think people wake up every morning with the intent to be negative. No matter how their day is going, they've just got to cause a ruckus. I work with a seasoned woman named "Nancy", and I absolutely hate to see her coming. All she does is wine and complain constantly, and hold other people accountable for her misfortunes. If she thinks that you are doing better than her or advancing, she will do whatever she can to hold you back.

But, the crazy part of the story is, I used to be friends with her. Before you say anything, at this point, I was no longer the negative person I used to be. In fact, I was trying to change her. Sadly, when a person has become settled in their ways, it takes a lot to remove them. Nancy is one of those people. What's even more alarming, is having worked with her for over 12 years, she's still negative. When she comes in to work, the first thing she does is readjust everyone's mood, except mine. Remember, I was once the bad guy, so I know the rules to the game she's playing.

However, I couldn't understand how someone could be 105 degrees at 8:00am in the morning, because she was anything but cool. If her computer didn't start, "Someone must've done something to it", she'd yell. If I listened to music at my desk, she'd report me, while hers blared loudly across the room. If you greeted her "Good Morning", it sent her over the edge, because clearly there was nothing good about her morning. Everybody tried to stay out of her way, because they were afraid of being caught in her storm.

She would often taunt, bully and pick on our colleagues, because she said "she could". However, because I was once where she was, I knew her pain was below the surface, and had nothing to do with us. Turns out, Nancy was subjecting everyone to her hurt and anguish, because she was miserable with her life. In her words, "she was old and had not accomplished the things she wanted, and when she saw others do it, she became angry". Rather than congratulate them on their success, she tried to ruin it. One thing I learned that day from Nancy, is that she didn't want anything out of life, except to destroy others. She had every opportunity she could to do better for herself, but she resigned to the idea that she was simply too old.

In fact, she wasn't too old, but she was too negative to see the good in anything, because she used to getting bad things. Many of our colleagues are young, as is I, but the difference between me and them, is they allowed what Nancy said to stop them from going any further, when all she did was push me farther away from her. That situation was very familiar, and reminded me of two ladies named Barbara and Jane.

Barbara and Jane had been friends for years, and no matter how many arguments or disagreements they had, they refused to let anything come between them....well, anything but success. You see, Barbara was more successful than Jane. Let's pretend for a moment, that money equates to success (in some people's eyes, this is true). Barbara is now higher up in the company, although they both started out at the bottom of the totem pole.

Prior to the promotion, both ladies struggled to make ends meet and worked tirelessly to climb their way up. Application after application, they applied and were denied. They always stated that if one was to come up before the other, they'd extend the hand to pull the other up. One day, God blessed Barbara with the opportunity of a lifetime, Chief Executive Officer. What a come up, but I don't think anyone was more happy for Barbara, than her good friend Jane.

Regardless of the power shift, they both remained the best of friends and continued to work well together. One day, Jane decided to pursue her dreams of becoming a business owner, and started her own writing company. Barbara told Jane that she'd do whatever she could to help her advance, because she wanted to see her succeed. At first, business was slow and although she wanted to give up, Jane continued to push through, because she knew that slow and steady wins the race!

Jane asked Barbara to allow her to do a presentation to the company, but it would be a separate charge, and not considered a part of her salary. Barbara obliged and told her that she'd even buy her books. Days, weeks and months went by, and Barbara didn't make good on her word. Unbeknownst to Jane, she'd get her opportunity of a lifetime, her very first paid speaking engagement that included a book signing. She was so happy, because her business was taking off, which meant more money for her.

Needless to say, not everyone was happy, especially Barbara. You see, she knew of Jane's gifts and there wasn't a doubt in her mind that she would do well and be successful, just as long as she wasn't more successful than her. Barbara didn't forget to ask the company to allow Jane to do a presentation, in fact, she deliberately didn't ask, because she knew it would open up doors for Jane. However, what she failed to realize is, she couldn't hold Jane back, because God was pushing her forward.

In case you haven't figured it out, I'm Jane, and at some point, you probably were too. A lot of people claim to be your friend or rally in your corner, but secretly, they want you to remain on their level or lower. They are negative and too bitter to enjoy their success, because they are desperately trying to keep you from achieving your own. They're envious and openly express their disgust of you climbing higher up the ladder of success over them. They'll pull, tug and grab on you in an attempts to bring you down, so you're unable to climb any higher.

However, what they don't understand is, God is the ladder and there's nothing they can do to stop Him from catapulting you higher! I'll never understand why someone would want to hinder my success or cause me to become stagnant, because they are fearful of me being better than them. I will never forget Barbara's ulterior motives, or what she potentially thought she could gain by not helping me.

If you ever run into a "Negative Nancy" or "Betraying Barbara", go the other way. These ladies are still crabs in the bucket, although they are free. However, they don't see that they are, because they are too busy trying to claw at you and hold you down. The hurtful words Nancy used and the mean things Barbara did could have been detrimental to me, but I didn't allow it, and neither should you. Keep going, it's only UP from here!

### Are you insulting or uplifting?

"If it weren't for you, I don't know where I'd be". "Your blog is so amazing and motivational, and it helps me get through what I am dealing with". "You're so inspiring and your messages always lift me up, when I am down". These are some of the statements that I frequently find in my message box from my followers. It's a good feeling when people pat me on the back, but there's no greater feeling than knowing how I have positively impacted the lives of so many people.

I take great joy in being inspiring and uplifting, because it is so easy to be insulting. Obviously I know, because I have insulted a lot of people. We don't realize how impactful or disserving our words can be to others, so before we speak, we should assess whether or not it will help or hurt. People want to know they can lean on others who can offer hope and motivation in their times of trouble. Nobody wants to hear, "That's what you get", especially when it's something they didn't deserve. We need to get in the habitat of raising others up, instead of putting them down, and keeping them there. Everyone makes mistakes, and no one should be held hostage to something they've done. Besides, they're already suffering enough, so don't continue to have dark clouds hanging over their heads. Be the sun they're looking for, but don't believe exists, because they've been in the dark for way too long. Let them know that no matter what they're going through, you're there, and make sure that you are.

Has there not been a time you were down on your luck and could really use some help? Maybe you are a domestic violence survivor, perhaps you were sexually abused or a recovering addict. Who knows what your situation is, or that of anyone else. It's during moments like these, that we need to be kind, thoughtful and uplifting to everyone, especially when we don't know the battles they're secretly fighting

Besides, one negative word to someone who already feels as though they have nothing to live for, could end it all, particularly their life. Do you want to be the one extending the hand, or the person looking up to grab it? Remember, it could always be you, so be careful how you treat people and watch your mouth!

**Stop it before it harvests**

If you have to ask yourself whether or not you should say something, or question if it would cause offense, then you probably shouldn't say anything at all. Then too, just because you have the thought doesn't make it right, nor give you the power to say whatever you want. You have the ability to stop your negative thinking before it harvests into something you regret planting. Although I know absolutely nothing about agriculture, what I do know is this, we are all farmers.

The hurtful words you use are the seeds you plant into the minds of others. Every day, you water them with insults, not to mention, mental, verbal and emotional abuse. Because of the negativity you feed them, they are unable to grow. Instead, they remain buried, which is essentially what you wanted anyway. Due to the lack of nutrients (positivity) they need, they aren't able to sprout. In fact, they aren't able to do anything, but to remain in the darkness you've subjected them too. They want to emerge, but don't know what they need to do to come out.

They could use a little sun (encouragement), but you've caused it not to shine. You are a bad farmer with no crops to harvest, because you've brought about one of the worst droughts there is, negativity. Your plants need hope, inspiration and praise to rain down on them, if they have any chance of blooming. Many have already died and withered away, as of result of your negligence.

That's it, you don't care! You don't care that someone's self-esteem has been lowered, because of the name calling. You don't care that someone sees themselves as worthless, because you told them they were. You don't care to think before you speak, because you want to give them a piece of your mind, or tell it like it is, whatever "it" may be. But, whatever that "it" is, do know you have the power to stop IT before it harvests? We're all familiar with the phrase, "Watch your thoughts, they become words: Watch your words, they become actions. Take heed and don't act first then think about what you've done later, because once the damage has been done, it can be incredibly hard to undo it.

## Steel weak

Cast iron ain't got nothing on me and wood breaks as soon as it's hit

Concrete is solid and aluminum foils, but I'm more powerful than all of it

People talk and when they do, I let them speak their mind

I would care about the things they say, but it doesn't bother me this time

The insults they hurl and negativity they throw, barely touches the surface

Hate is strong, but it doesn't affect me, so what exactly is its purpose?

The attacks keep coming and because I'm resilient, I keep on bouncing back

No matter the weapon they use against me, they'll never be my match

They spread rumors, employ lies and drag me through the dirt

But because I'm not the least bit affected, none of their antics hurt

I can take anything that comes my way, so shoot your best shot

If name calling is the best you have, then nothing is all you've got

Titanium is tough, but I'm tougher, and can withstand any level of heat

Although I'm made of stainless steel, sometimes I do get weak

No matter how much we proclaim words don't have any power, they do. They have the power to hurt you, damage you and destroy you. They have the power to influence you, change your perception of people and alter who you are as a person. They have the power to distort your thinking and make you feel your life is over, when it's far from done. Words are the most effective weapon used to take away your peace, lower your self-esteem, and decrease your value to the point you question whether or not you were ever worth anything to begin with. Words can make or break you; will you let them?

Have you ever met someone who swore they were made of steel and nothing could hurt them? It didn't matter what someone said or did, because they were completely "unbothered". Well, I'm that someone, and I am tired of pretending. I'm tired of pretending I don't care. I'm tired of pretending I'm strong. I'm tired of pretending "it" doesn't bother me. I'm tired of pretending words don't hurt me, when they do. In fact, all of it does. I have lived a lie for a very long time. I was perfectly okay with it, because it meant I didn't have to face the truth, and the fact that it hurts.

I write to inspire others and offer hope, but sometimes I need the strength of my words to hold me up, when I can no longer do it myself. I tend to carry loads in excess of hurt, problems (most not my own) and pain that I've experienced over the course of my life. Still thinking I'm made of steel, I continue to maintain my tough exterior and the ability to withstand *anything*, when on the inside, I'm dying from *everything*. Will I survive? Where is the resilience I proudly boast of?

I thought I was Superwoman and could take anything negative someone threw at me, but because my cape is gone, I can't fly away even if I wanted to. I hate to admit it, but I am weak and my superpowers cease to exist. I am vulnerable, and it's scary, because now I'm susceptible to everything, when I told myself I wasn't. However, I have decided, that none of it matters, because I'm done pretending! There's a person I've allowed to belittle me for years. I didn't understand the reason for their dislike and hate towards me. In the beginning, I fought back, and said whatever I could to hurt this person, because they had done it to me. But, when I saw how pointless it was, I refrained from speaking.

I didn't give them the satisfaction of knowing I was hurting on the inside, because then they'd win. This abuse continued, and I often wondered why I was the only one being treated this way. Out of all the people they could hate, I had to be the one. I had to be the "ugly" one. I had to be the "black" one. I had to be whatever they called me, because that's what they thought of me. I began to internalize a lot of things and questioned if I'd get past the hurt or live in it. So, I poked out my steel chest, and carried on with my life, and brought the hurt and pain with me.

I tried to let it go, by letting them go, but God would convict me every time. I tried to make things right, but I couldn't, nor could I correct an error that felt as though it wasn't wrong. I asked someone to intervene and meet with us both, but even that didn't work. After wrecking my brain with thoughts of what I could have possibly done wrong, I realized I hadn't. More than anything, it was them. Obviously they were battling with issues unknown to me, or anyone for that matter. Rather than reach out for help, they chose to do only what they could to ease the pain, and that was to inflict it upon someone else, and that someone was me.

No longer accepting their behavior, I started to distance myself, because I just could not be around that type of negativity. To be honest, it threatened my peace of mind and had I let it continue, it probably would've destroyed me, considering how weak I had become. As I've mentioned, you will have haters, bullies and people that are mean for no reason at all, but don't you become one of those people. I could've very easily let the negative things this person said define who I am, and more importantly, make me like them.

Not to make any excuses, but I stopped being affected by this person's actions, because clearly they were being effected by something. I was once on both ends of the spectrum, so I know what it's like to be the bully and the one being bullied. The turning point for me, was when I chose to change their narrative of me. I gave myself positive affirmations daily, because I knew who I was and it was not the disgust they made me feel, as a result of the filthy things they said about me. Besides, I am not the "ugly" one, because I know I'm beautiful. I am not the "black" one, but the brown skinned girl. I am not (always) tough, and that's okay.

However, what's not okay is someone belittling you and making you feel any less than human. You are more than what your aggressor says you are. Live in your truth, and refuse to believe their lies. Be the reason for someone else's strength, because sometimes, it takes them seeing you do it, so they know it can be done.

### Silence is a response

A lot of times, you're going to find yourself in situations that require you to "speak now or forever hold your peace". This may prove to be very difficult, especially for someone who doesn't like keeping quiet or turning the other cheek. When insulted, our *hurt feelings* command that we get them back for what they did, but why is retaliation the first line of defense? There are other ways to fight back, besides using your tongue, and silence is one of them. Granted it might not be your first choice, but it'll certainly be the best, and probably the one they're least expecting.

Quite naturally, when people are arguing or having a difference of opinion, the goal is to get their point across. It doesn't matter if they have to shout to the rooftops or threaten to move mountains to be heard, as long as their point is made and received. However, I have perfected the art of hearing and not listening. I can *hear* someone spewing negativity and hate. I can *hear* them be confrontational with me, and I can *hear* them attempt to harm me with their words. But, the beauty in having ears, is that I get to control what I *listen* to.

Although I can hear everything someone says to me, I don't listen to shit they have to say. That's my choice and ultimately, the decision I always make. I think many people don't realize they have that option or privilege I should say, because it has been taken away from them. However, everyone has a choice, so whether you choose to make one or not, is totally up to you. Whichever avenue you take, should be depended upon your feelings to the situation. If you're vindictive, petty and want to be heard, you're going to *choose* to stay and fight.

On the other hand, if you can be seen and not heard, you won't mind keeping quiet, because the true power lies in what you don't say. Besides, don't allow their words to poke you and more importantly, provoke you. Remember, if there is no battle, there is no need for you to fight. However, if you are met with one, be smart when you choose your weapon. There are some things that are not worth your time or energy, although it can be difficult not to react. Before you decide to lodge your attack, think about it and ask yourself, "What is this going to change"?

I know you're probably still fighting me on this one, but don't. Your voice doesn't need to be heard, so people will know that you're in the room. Your presence took care of that the moment you walked in. Ponder on this, which is more harmful? Your retaliation, or their threat? They may say something that is very minute, but you may respond in a more monstrous way. For example, if someone says they don't like my hair, because it's ugly. I'm not going to threaten to beat them up, because their opinion is minor, petty and doesn't have any bearing on me at all. What I will do, however, is ignore that person, because if they don't have an audience, then they can't put on a show. Besides, no one needs to see their performance anyway. Sometimes, it's going to take you showing people that you can fight back without using your hands or words, and silence is the ultimate response.

### Walk, even if you are alone

Have you ever backed down from a fight? If not, did your ego get in the way, or was it because you had something to prove? Moreover, you had a reputation to uphold, because *everybody* knows not to mess with you. After the dust settled, did you question your actions or think what would've happened had you chosen to just walk away? Being the bigger person can be difficult at times, and taking the high road isn't always the *way to go*. I know, because I've very seldom traveled it.

However, when I'm affronted by someone, being combative is no longer my choice of weapon, walking is. I mentally exit the situation first, and then I physically follow. Quite naturally, the aggressor will think their intimidation has caused them to win, when all it did was make them a loser. Walking away is not easy, but it's what's best, not just for you, but the other person as well. I'm confident that if they see me walk away, they'll back down and eventually do the same.

## Understanding the power of words

Fat, ugly and bald-headed, are some pretty powerful and tasteless words. In fact, they are so powerful, I allowed them to hurt me and reconstruct my whole life and well-being, but not for the better. Instead, I agreed, because after all, I was (still am) overweight, have always had a short amount of hair and didn't necessarily consider myself eye candy. Despite all of that, I did however, consider my best feature to be my smile, but even it went away when people told me I didn't have a reason to. I was in bad shape, and didn't know if I'd ever go back to who I was, or remain the person they formed me to be.

I felt lost, hopeless and abandoned, because I was hurting and in desperate need of saving, but there wasn't a rescue crew in sight. People, mean words, and negativity (coupled with many other things), stole my childhood and threatened to do the same to my adult life, and because of my fragileness, it did. Regardless of what I was going through, I always put on a façade and had people envying the strength and confidence they thought I had, but ultimately lacked. However, by the end of the day, I'd remove the mask and was forced to look at the scars *they* gave me.

All of my bruises, sores and cuts were emotional and mental, so physically I appeared and looked fine. However, I was far from it. I was on the verge of a nervous fucking breakdown, and I knew once I hit rock bottom, there was no coming back. Truthfully, it wouldn't have mattered anyway, because I was already *dead*. I allowed all that shit to *kill* my spirit, rob me of my joy and screw with my peace of mind. I guess I considered it to be the ultimate payback, my payback, for all the people who'd been victims of my wrath. I felt like I was on an episode of *Bugs Bunny*, because suddenly the "rabbit had the gun".

All I could do was throw my hands up and say, "Okay, you've got me. You win". But, as Nene Leakes would say, "You'll never win, playing dirty". In fact, no one does. It doesn't matter what someone says to you, regardless of how bad it hurts, don't react. After all, that's the goal of the aggressor. They want to see how far they can throw the ball, before it hits you. No matter what they pitch, don't swing your bat! In fact, just leave the game. I've heard people say, "I don't see how someone can get offended by what someone says to them, because words are just words". Honestly, they're not. They're powerful, detrimental, ammunition, destructive and damaging. It's important to be mindful of the things we say, because some people are literally hanging by a thread, and you could be the reason it snaps.

If you are like I once was, I hope this book offers you enough insight on how the negativity you spew impacts not only the person you attack, but their life. People, particularly children, who are subjected to bullying, have been known to commit suicide, because they've allowed people like you (and me) to get to them. Due to the overwhelming pressure mounting against them, they collapse, and don't ever get back up. Don't start a fire and continue to fuel it, because you want to see how much heat one can withstand. Think about it before you speak about it and understand there lies great power in your words.

**About the Author**

Deetra La'Rue Benn is a 35-year-old Writer, Author and Motivational Speaker, from Montgomery, AL. She started out writing poetry, but God lead her to write inspirational books to offer support to those in need. She's the author of ***Glitter but no gold: How I turned my wounds into wisdom, Let's TALK! Conversations that need to be had, but often go undone and Words are weapons too! (Understanding the power of words).*** She is a graduate of Troy University, with a BS in Political Science and an MS in Counseling/Psy. Currently, she serves as the Director of Student Support Services (**TRiO**) at the Troy Montgomery Campus. Deetra enjoys volunteering, giving back to the community, shopping, family, and connecting with others through her motivational website, ***Notes by La'Rue (www.notesbylarue.com)***, where she brings hope, encouragement and motivation, one **"note"** at a time.

www.ingramcontent.com/pod-product-compliance
Lightning Source LLC
LaVergne TN
LVHW041238080426
835508LV00011B/1273